The Road Trip Cookbook: World Famous Drive-ins, Diners and Dive Recipes from Route 66

Table of Contents

Baby Back Ribs

Serves: 2
Cooking Time: 18 hours

Ingredients

Rub
1 cup sugar, turbinado
¼ cup salt
6 tbsp paprika
4 tbsp chili powder
2 tbsp garlic powder
1 tbsp onion powder
2 tsp cumin
2 tsp powdered mustard
1 ½ tsp pepper, cayenne
1 tsp salt and pepper to taste

Ribs
1 to 2 ½ lb slab of ribs
2 tbsp mustard
2 tbsp BBQ sauce

Directions

I. Mix the dry ingredients (the rub) and add all of the ingredients to a container with a lid, shake and wait. Do this one day ahead of time, if possible.
II. Lay the ribs out with the curve side facing up. Pull out the membrane.
III. Sprinkle about 1 tsp of rub over the side of the ribs, then cover with yellow mustard. The mustard will help to spread the rub around.

IV. Repeat the last two steps until you have covered the entire slab of ribs.
V.   Set the ribs on a tray and leave them in the refrigerator overnight.
VI. Set a smoker to 200 °F, use apple or cherry wood for added flavor.
VII. Set the ribs in the smoker, curve side down and smoke for 2 hours.
VIII. After 2 hours, raise the temperature to 250 °F for another 2 ½ hours.
IX. When the bones are ready to pull apart, they are almost done. Smoke for about another half an hour if they don't pull apart.
X.   Remove the meat from the smoker and spread BBQ sauce over the ribs before serving (optional).

Nutritional Information

Calories 662, Fat 42.4g, Carbohydrates 48.6g, Protein 28.4g

Serves: 2
Cooking Time: 15 minutes

Ingredients

½ lb shrimp
artichokes, halved, cooked
2 oz tomatoes, diced
1 package pasta, fettuccini
2 oz wine, sherry
1 oz heavy cream
1 oz butter
2 oz butter, herb

Directions

I. Cover the shrimp in flour and heat in a skillet on medium to high heat, cook until they are a golden color.
II. Add in the remaining ingredients and cook for another 1 to 2 minutes, let the sauce and shrimp thicken.
III. Cook the pasta according to the package directions.
IV. Stir shrimp and sauce in with the pasta.

Nutritional Information

Calories 275, Fat 9.7g, Carbohydrates 27.9g, Protein 16.8g

Route 66 Diner Peach Cobbler

Serves: 20
Cooking Time: 1 hour

Ingredients

1 can peaches, sliced, drained
3/4 cup peach juice
1/2 cup brown sugar
2 tbsp cornstarch
1/8 tsp cinnamon
1 cup flour
1 tsp baking soda
1/2 stick butter
ice cream, vanilla, garnish

Directions

I. Lay the peaches along the bottom of the baking dish and save the juice.
II. Pour the peach juice into a saucepan, add the brown sugar, cornstarch and cinnamon, cook over low to medium heat until everything thickens.
III. Pour the thickened peach juice over the peaches in the baking dish.
IV. Stir in the flour, baking soda and remaining ingredients in a mixing bowl until you have a nice crumbly texture.
V. Sprinkle this crumbly dough over the peach mix. Set a few drops of butter throughout the dish to keep the dough from drying out during baking.
VI. Bake for about 35 to 40 minutes at 350 °F. Watch for it to become a golden brown along the top and for the peach mix to start bubbling. That is a sign that it is done.

VII.   Remove, let cool and serve with vanilla ice cream.

Nutritional Information

Calories 190, Fat 7.9g, Carbohydrates 31.3g, Protein 2.3g

Serves: 7 to 8 dz cookies
Cooking Time: 1 hour and 20 minutes

Ingredients

1 cup butter

1 cup sugar

½ cup sugar, powdered

¾ cup corn oil

½ cup maple syrup

2 eggs

1 tsp baking soda

1 tsp cream of tarter

½ tsp salt

4 cups flour

Directions

I.   Cream the butter and both of the sugars, then stir in the oil, syrup, eggs and cream.
II. In a separate bowl, sift the dry ingredients.
III. Fold together both bowls of ingredients and stir until you have a thick dough.
IV. Chill the dough in the fridge for about an hour.
V.   Drop by the spoonful on a greased cookie sheet and bake for 10 to 12 minutes at 350 °F.
VI. Cool before serving.

Nutritional Information

Calories 111, Fat 6.1g, Carbohydrates 13.6g, Protein 1.5g

Route 66 Diner-Style French Toast

Serves: 4
Cooking Time: 30 minutes

Ingredients

- 1 cup flour, sifted
- 1 tsp baking powder
- 1 tsp salt
- 2 eggs
- 1 cup milk
- 2 tbsp vegetable oil
- 6 to 8 slices French Cinnamon Raisin Bread

Directions

I. In a large mixing bowl, combine the eggs, milk and oil, stir in the flour and baking soda.
II. Dip the bread into the mix until each piece is completely coated.
III. Add each piece (I suggest cooking them one at a time) to the skillet and cook until completely fried on each side.
IV. Serve warm with syrup.

Nutritional Information

Calories 166, Fat 3.4g, Carbohydrates 27.9g, Protein 5.1g

Serves: 6 to 8
Cooking Time: 45 minutes

Ingredients

2 lbs shrimp, raw, prepared
4 jalapeño, minced
4 tbsp cilantro, chopped
2 tbsp garlic, minced
1 lime, juiced
1 tsp salt

Buttermilk Batter

2 cups cornmeal, yellow
1 cup flour
3 tbsp sugar
1 ½ tbsp baking powder
1 tbsp cilantro, chopped
1 tbsp salt
2 ½ cups buttermilk
eggs

Directions

I. Combine the shrimp with all of the ingredients and grind through a food processor.
II. Shape the ground shrimp mixture into large balls and skewer each one of the balls (they should look like hotdogs on a stick or corn dogs).
III. Line a baking sheet with the skewered shrimp dogs and freeze them.

IV.   Add all of the dry ingredients for the batter to a bowl and mix really well.
V.   Add the remaining ingredients until you have a creamy, batter substance.
VI.   Heat a deep fryer or skillet with oil. Fry these one at a time.
VII.   Dip each of the frozen, skewer sticks into the batter and fry for about 8 to 10 minutes or until the batter becomes a dark-golden color.

Nutritional Information

Calories 81, Fat 21.7g, Carbohydrates 14.6g, Protein 1.1g

Serves: 2
Cooking Time: 30 to 45 minutes

Ingredients

1 large trout, prepared for grilling
lemon pepper and salt to taste
1 cup rice, cooked
corn husks
2 tbsp butter
¼ tsp parsley flakes
¼ tsp garlic powder
¼ tsp onion powder
½ tsp lemon juice
1 drop liquid smoke
1 tsp Worcestershire sauce

Directions

I.   Season the trout with the lemon pepper and salt.
II. Stuff the trout's belly with rice and wrap the trout with corn husks, then wrap in aluminum foil.
III. Mix the butter with the remaining ingredients and pour over the trout and corn husks. Also wrap that in foil. This helps keep the sauce from leaking out.
IV. Set the foil-wrapped trout and husks over heat (grill or campfire).
V.   Grill for 10 to 12 minutes.

Nutritional Information

Calories 28.3, Fat .3g, Carbohydrates 6g, Protein .7g

Makes: 2 cups
Cooking Time: 30 minutes

Ingredients

1 onion, diced
3 tomatoes, diced
2 chilies, yellow, minced
3 tbsp cilantro, chopped
garlic powder
salt to taste

Directions

I.   Combine everything together.
II.   Set in the fridge until it is ready to serve.

Nutritional Information

Calories 23, Fat 1.5g, Carbohydrates 7.6g, Protein 29.4g

Makes: 2 ½ cups
Cooking Time: 30 minutes

Ingredients

3 Haas avocadoes
1 tbsp water
1 tomato, diced
1 onion, diced
salt

Directions

I.   Scoop the avocadoes and mash the "meat."
II. Transfer the avocado filling to a bowl and stir in the water and remaining ingredients.
III. Season with salt to taste.

Nutritional Information

Calories 150, Fat 5.7g, Carbohydrates 20.2g, Protein 6.3g

Serves: 1
Cooking Time: 30 minutes

Ingredients

8 oz ground beef
4 slices cheese, American
2 slices onion, red
4 slices of tomato, thick
lettuce
burger garnishes: ketchup, mustard, mayo, etc.

Directions

I.   Make two patties with the 8 oz ground beef and grill the patties over a skillet or on the grill.
II.   Once cooked to desired tenderness, set aside.
III. Toast both insides of the burger buns.
IV.   Assemble the burger with patties, cheese and garnishes.

Nutritional Information

Calories 550, Fat 20.4g, Carbohydrates 55.2g, Protein 38.9g

Serves: 14 to 16
Cooking Time: 4 hours

Ingredients

20 lbs chili meat (of your choice)
2 10 lbs cans tomato sauce
12 tbsp chili powder
6 tbsp chili flakes, crushed
2 tbsp salt and pepper to taste
3 tbsp garlic
2 tsp oregano
2 tsp cumin
15 tbsp paprika
8 cups onion, fresh, diced
cooked beans (side dish)

Directions

I.   Add the meat to a large roaster pan and brown it at 450 °F, stir often.
II. Stir in the remaining ingredients and lower the temperature to 375 °F, cover and bake for about 3 hours.
III. When it is done cooking, you can freeze it in smaller batches, if desired.
IV. Serve with freshly-cooked beans.

Nutritional Information

Calories 256, Fat 15.6g, Carbohydrates 13.4g, Protein 16.3g

Serves: 4
Cooking Time: 30 to 45 minutes

Ingredients

1 cup walnuts
3/4 cup beans, garbanzo
1/3 cup bread crumbs, dried
1 tbsp grill seasoning
1 tsp smoked paprika
1/4 tsp pepper, red, flakes
1 tbsp cider vinegar
1 tbsp olive oil
1 egg, whisked
hamburger buns
lettuce, tomato and other burger garnishes
mayo or honey mustard

Directions

I.   These diner burgers are best on the grill.
II.   In a blender or food processor, combine the walnuts, beans, bread crumbs, seasonings, oil and vinegar, pulse.
III.   Throw in the whisked egg and pulse for another 12 to 15 seconds.
IV.   Take the mix from the blender, divide into 4 sections and make small, round balls. Press into the center of each of the 4 round balls.
V.   Cook the burgers over the grill to the desired tenderness. Once they are cooked, add cheese over the top long enough for the cheese to melt.
VI.   Remove from the heat and assemble burgers with garnishes.

Nutritional Information

Calories 404, Fat 33.5g, Carbohydrates 2.7g, Protein 20.9g

Orange Smoothie

Serves: 4
Cooking Time: 5 minutes

Ingredients

8 oz orange juice, frozen
1 oz pudding mix, vanilla
1 yogurt, orange cream
1 cup milk
¼ cup flavor liqueur, orange flavor
2 cups ice

Directions

Add everything into a food processor or blender and blend until it is smooth and creamy.

Nutritional Information

Calories 107, Fat 1.3g, Carbohydrates 23.4g, Protein 1.7g

Mini Corn Dogs with Pepper Relish

Serves: 4
Cooking Time: 30 minutes

Ingredients

Spicy Pickle Sauce

¾ cup ketchup
¼ cup hot peppers, pickled, diced
¼ cup sweet peppers, pickled, diced

Dogs

1 egg
1 package corn muffin mix
2 tsp garlic powder
2 tsp onion powder
¾ cup milk
½ cup flour
1 package mini franks
shortening or oil

Directions

I. Mix the pickle relish dipping sauce. Once it is well blended, set aside until ready to serve.
II. In a separate, large bowl, combine everything but the cocktail franks and frying oil.
III. Skewer the franks and heat the oil for frying.
IV. Dip the franks in the batter and fry for about 1 to 2 minutes. They should be a golden-brown color. Drain the excess grease with a paper-towel lined plate.
V. Serve corn dogs with the spicy pickle sauce.

Nutritional Information

Calories 81, Fat 21.7g, Carbohydrates 14.6g, Protein 1.1g

Serves: 4
Cooking Time: 1 hour and 15 minutes

Ingredients

3 bottles root beer
¼ cup sugar

Sundae

1 qt ice cream, vanilla
hard candies, root beer
1 cup whipped cream
3 sugar cones, crumbs
cherries

Directions

I. Boil the sugar and root beer in a medium size saucepan. Once it is boiling, reduce and simmer for about 45 minutes. The mix should dissolve down to about ¾ and it should be syrupy. Once this happens, remove from the heat.
II. Put the candies in a Ziploc® baggie and crush them.
III. Add the ice cream to the dishes and scoop the root beer syrup over the ice cream, add cool whip.
IV. Sprinkle the candy over the cool whip, then the sugar-cone crumbs, followed by a cherry on top.

Nutritional Information

Calories 147, Fat 1g, Carbohydrates 41.2g, Protein 1.7g

Cheese Fries

Serves: 4
Cooking Time: 10 minutes

Ingredients

- 1 bag fries, wedges, frozen
- 1 tbsp chili seasoning
- 1 can chili
- 1 package cheese, shredded
- 1 onion, green, sliced
- 2 tbsp sour cream

Directions

I. Heat the grill to a medium heat.
II. In a bowl, combine the fries and chili seasoning, toss to make sure the fries are well coated.
III. Add the fries to the grill (in aluminum foil or a grilling pan) and grill for about 4 minutes, turn and grill on the other side for 4 minutes.
IV. While the fries are cooking, cook the chili in a medium-size saucepan and bring to a simmer.
V. Take the fries off the grill once they are cooked thoroughly.
VI. Move the cooked fries to a serving dish and pour the cooked chili over the top of the fries.
VII. Sprinkle shredded cheese and onions over the top of the chili.

Nutritional Information

Calories 171, Fat 6.2g, Carbohydrates 23.1g, Protein 9.2g

Cheesy Grub Sandwich

Serves: 4
Cooking Time: 35 to 40 minutes

Ingredients

1 lb ground beef
2 tsp Montreal steak seasoning
1 tsp Worcestershire sauce
2 tbsp butter
2 tbsp flour
¾ cup milk
1 cup cheese, shredded
salt and pepper to taste

Directions

I.   Season the beef and brown in a skillet. Stir in the Worcestershire sauce as the beef is browning.
II.   Drain off the excess grease and set the skillet aside.
III. In a smaller saucepan, melt the butter, stir in the flour and whisk together.
IV.   Let the flour and butter cook for about 2 to 3 minutes.
V.   Whisk in the milk and bring everything to a boil. Wait for the sauce to thicken and remove it from the heat.
VI.   Stir in the cheese until it is melted.
VII. Season with salt and pepper to taste.
VIII. Pour the cheese over the seasoned, cooked ground beef.
IX.   Add cheesy beef to hot dog buns and serve.

Nutritional Information

Calories 360, Fat 5.4g, Carbohydrates 47.3g, Protein 32.6g

Fountain Style Milkshake

Serves: 1
Cooking Time: 10 minutes

Ingredients

½ cup milk
¼ cup water, carbonated
3 tbsp malted milk powder
½ tsp vanilla
2 cups ice cream, vanilla

Directions

Blend all of the ingredients together until everything is smooth and creamy.

Nutritional Information

Calories 307, Fat 16.4g, Carbohydrates 42g, Protein 42g

Serves: 1
Cooking Time: 10 minutes

Ingredients

4 cups ice cream, chocolate
2 cups milk
¼ cup sugar, brown
¼ cup sugar, granulated
¼ cup cinnamon, ground

Directions

I.   Add everything to a blender or food processor and blend until smooth.
II. Pour into large mug (frosted is best).

Nutritional Information

Calories 161, Fat 14.7g, Carbohydrates 13.4g, Protein 22g

Cream Soda

Serves: 1
Cooking Time: 10 minutes

Ingredients

3 oz water, carbonated
3/4 oz syrup, passion fruit
3/4 oz syrup, watermelon
1 oz half & half

Directions

I.   Fill a frosted glass 1/2 way full with ice.
II.   Fill 2/3 way full with carbonated water and add the syrups.
III. Carefully stir in the half & half as the last ingredient.
IV.   Stir as you drink or when ready to serve.

Nutritional Information

Calories 39, Fat 3.5g, Carbohydrates 2.3g, Protein .9g

Serves: 3
Cooking Time: 5 minutes

Ingredients

1 cup ice cream, vanilla
¾ cup ice cream, chocolate
¾ cup ice cream, strawberry
½ cup buttermilk
½ cup milk, chocolate
1 tbsp powder, malted milk

Directions

I.	Combine all of the ice cream together with the other listed ingredients. Mix on high until smooth and creamy. This could take about 2 minutes.
II.	Pour into three serving glasses (frosted is best).

Nutritional Information

Calories 126, Fat .6g, Carbohydrates 24.5g, Protein 6.8g

Serves: 1
Cooking Time: 5 minutes

Ingredients

4 scoops ice cream, vanilla
¼ cup milk
¼ cup syrup, chocolate
1 to 2 drops mint extract

Directions

I.   Add everything into the blender and blend until smooth and creamy.
II.   Serve in a frosted glass.

Nutritional Information

Calories 330, Fat 1.5g, Carbohydrates 71.6g, Protein 10.2g

Serves: 1
Cooking Time: 45 minutes

Ingredients

2 cups crumbs, graham cracker
½ cup sugar
½ cup butter
1 package cream cheese, soft
1 cup sugar
1 tsp vanilla
3 bananas, sliced
1 can pineapple, crushed
1 container cool whip
½ cup pecans or peanuts, chopped
1 jar cherries

Directions

I.   Preheat the oven to 350 °F.
II. Melt butter in a skillet over low heat.
III. Remove the pan from the heat, add in ½ cup sugar and the graham cracker crumbs. Press the crust down into a pie pan and bake for 10 to 15 minutes.
IV. Cream together the cream cheese, 1 cup sugar and the vanilla, spread over the crust.
V.   Layer the bananas, pineapple and whipped cream over the bars, in the order listed. Sprinkle nuts and cherries over the top.
VI. Let it sit in the fridge for at least 6 hours or overnight, if possible.
VII. Cut into serving squares.

Nutritional Information

Calories 158, Fat 4.2g, Carbohydrates 25.8g, Protein 3.8g

Printed in Great Britain
by Amazon